4-Chord Guitar Songs
for the Absolute Beginner

30 songs with only 4 chords!

National Guitar Workshop Book

Approved Curriculum

W9-BRI-586

Susan Mazer

Alfred, the leader in educational publishing, and the National Guitar Workshop, one of America's finest guitar schools, have joined forces to bring you the best, most progressive educational tools possible. We hope you will enjoy this book and encourage you to look for other fine products from Alfred and the National Guitar Workshop.

Alfred Publishing Co., Inc.
16320 Roscoe Blvd., Suite 100
P.O. Box 10003
Van Nuys, CA 91410-0003
alfred.com

ISBN-10: 0-7390-5274-8 (Book and CD)
ISBN-13: 978-0-7390-5274-7 (Book and CD)

*This book was acquired, edited and produced by Workshop Arts, Inc., the publishing arm of the National Guitar Workshop.
Nathaniel Gunod, acquisitions, managing editor
Burgess Speed, acquisitions, senior editor
Matthew Liston, editor, music typesetter
Timothy Phelps, interior design
CD recorded by Mark Schane-Lydon at WorkshopLive.com, Pittsfield, MA
Susan Mazer (guitar and vocals), Joe Grieco (vocals),
Dan Hofmann (vocals, tracks 8 and 9)*

*Cover photos: Dry Lake Bed © Photodisc, Inc.; Hatching © West Stock, Inc.
Cover guitar courtesy of Taylor Guitars*

Table of Contents

A Note on Public Domain Material

This book contains a number of traditional tunes and folk songs. Although reference is made to artists who have recorded and copyrighted their own versions of these songs, what appears in this book is the original public domain material.

About the Author

Philadelphia-born *Susan Mazer* lives and works in Connecticut. She received her bachelor of music degree from the Hartt School of Music. Susan is on the faculty at the Hartford Conservatory, where she teaches theory and ear training, and was also the first female guitar instructor to teach at the National Guitar Workshop. Susan has been performing for the last 20 years and now plays with the Keith and Mazer Trio. The author of several instructional books, including the best-selling *Guitar for the Absolute Beginner* (Alfred/National Guitar Workshop #20421), Susan also teaches online guitar lessons at WorkshopLive.com.

PHOTO BY CHRISTOPHER PECK

● Acknowledgements

Thank you to Barbara Gunterman, Joe Keith, Megan Keith, David Keith, Jean, Carol, The Music Shop in Southington, Hartford Conservatory, Mark Schane-Lydon, Burgess Speed, Timothy Phelps, Mindy, Mom, my father's spirit, and all my wonderful students.

● Dedication

Thank you to Dave and Nat for your friendship and for giving me all the wonderful opportunities over the years.

A compact disc is included with this book. This disc can make learning with the book easier and more enjoyable. The symbol shown at the left appears next to every song that is on the CD. Use the CD to help ensure that you're capturing the feel of the songs and interpreting the rhythms correctly. The track number below the symbol corresponds directly to the song you want to hear. Some of the songs are recorded in their entirety, while others include only the first verses and choruses. Track 1 is a tuning track that will help you tune your guitar to this CD.

How to Use This Book

This songbook is intended for beginning guitar players of every age, but can be used by players of any skill level. The great news, if you are an absolute beginner, is that there are thousands of songs you can play with just three or four chords. This book is a great place to start learning these songs because: 1) It features a wide range of material, from the most current rock tunes to traditional folk songs of the 1920s, and, 2) It includes simplified chord forms and strumming patterns that will help the beginner sound great playing these songs. If you're jamming with friends, doing a sing-along, or just playing by yourself, you'll find these tunes fun and easy to play. Although you don't need to know how to read music to use this book, you do need to know the basics of guitar playing. To learn these basics, check out *Guitar for the Absolute Beginner Complete* (Alfred/NGW #27815) for a full and easy introductory course. Enjoy!

How Do I Read the Chord Diagrams?

A *chord diagram* is shown to the right. The vertical lines represent the strings of the guitar. The horizontal lines represent frets. The numbers down the left side of the diagram tell you the fret numbers. The row of numbers along the top tell you which left-hand fingers to use for each string. The number 0 indicates an open string, and an x indicates you should not play that string. The dark circles show you where to place each finger on the fretboard.

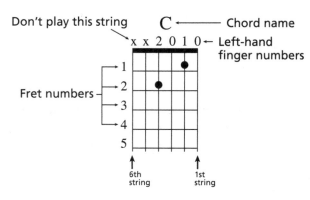

How Do I Know What to Play with My Right Hand?

Unfortunately for all beginning and intermediate students, most books don't tell you which strumming pattern to use for each song. That's partially because the right-hand pattern is sometimes a matter of preference. In this book, the strumming patterns are at the top of each page. *Rhythmic notation* is used to indicate the strumming patterns. This type of notation only indicates the rhythm to be played, but not specific notes.

Rhythmic Notation

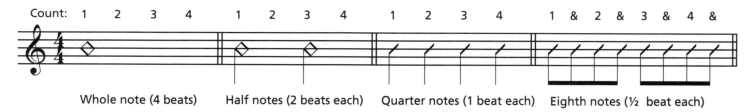

The Strumming Patterns

To the right is an example of a strumming pattern. Strum the chords in the song down (⊓) and up (∨) as indicated. Notice in this pattern, there is a *tie* connecting the second and third eighth-note strums. This tells you to let the first strum ring out for the value of the two strums combined. If this sounds complicated, don't worry. Just listen to the CD to be sure you're getting the strums right.

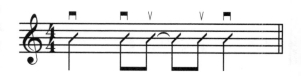

The Bass-Strum Technique

To the right is a pattern using the *bass-strum technique.* The first note in the pattern has a stem going upward and it is labeled "bass." This tells you to play the lowest note of the chord by itself, then strum the remaining strings for the rest of the pattern. For example, if you were applying this pattern to the C chord at the top of the page, you would play the note on the 4th string 2nd fret by itself on beat 1, then strum the rest of the chord on beats 2 and 3.

What Can I Do if I Have Trouble Singing and Playing at the Same Time?

For most people, it's difficult to concentrate on two things at once. That means either the singing or the playing has to be on "autopilot." Here are some steps you can take to learn how to sing and play at the same time.

1. Learn the strumming pattern so you can play without giving it any thought. You should be able to talk on the phone, or watch TV, and still keep the right-hand pattern going.

2. Let someone else sing while you play (or play along with the accompanying CD), so you can hear how the vocal line goes with the guitar part.

3. Learn to "audiate," or "think the music," in your head while you play.

4. Play the guitar and just speak the words with rhythm. Don't worry about singing.

5. Finally, sing and play together. Try not to think too much. Sometimes, if you just "go for it," you play better. If you're having trouble, go measure by measure. Remember that your right hand and your vocal line don't always match up. Sometimes, you're strumming without singing any words, and sometimes you're singing between strums.

Don't get frustrated. It will come in time!

What if the Song Is in the Wrong Range for My Voice?

Everybody's voice has a different range. Some people sing high and some people sing lower. Changing the *key*, or tonal center, doesn't really affect the melody of the song at all. You can sing "Happy Birthday" in any key and it still sounds like "Happy Birthday." If you find that a song is not in your vocal range, try using a *capo*, which is a metal bar that clamps your strings down at a particular fret, effectively changing the range of the guitar while allowing you to use the same chord forms. Use trial and error to find the fret that is right for your voice. This process is called *transposition*, which means keeping the same pattern of chords, but moving them to another key.

You can also transpose without using a capo by changing the chords. The chart below will help you in this process. If you are in the key of A, find it on the first line of the chart, then read horizontally to find the chords in the key. Let's say that the song uses the chords A, D, E. If you want to change the key to D, go down two lines to the key of D. Then, read across horizontally to find the chords in the same position. A, D, and E will now be D, G, and A.

When transposing to a different key, chords keep their *quality*, or type. Major chords stay major in the new key, 7th chords remain 7th chords, and minor chords become minor chords. So, A, D, and E7 in the key of A becomes D, G, and A7 in the key of D.

The chart to the right shows the six keys that are most commonly played by beginning guitarists, as well as the most commonly-used chords in each of those keys.

KEY	CHORDS					
A	A	Bmin	C#min	D	E	F#min
C	C	Dmin	Emin	F	G	Amin
D	D	Emin	F#min	G	A	Bmin
E	E	F#min	G#min	A	B	C#min
F	F	Gmin	Amin	B♭	C	Dmin
G	G	Amin	Bmin	C	D	Emin

What Are the Parts of a Song?

Intro: A short beginning, or preparatory, section of a song.

Verse: The part of a song that moves the "story" forward. The lyrics change with each new verse.

Chorus: The refrain, or part of the song that repeats while alternating with changing verses.

Pre-chorus: Short section of a song that leads into the chorus.

Outro: Section that concludes a song.

SECTION ONE: Pop/Rock Songs

Rock 'n' roll is rooted in the blues and traditional spirituals. Even though most pop and rock tunes may sound complicated, they do not use more than a few basic chords. This section features some great tunes that span the history of this genre. Let's get started!

Good Riddance (Time of Your Life)

Lyrics by BILLIE JOE
Music by BILLIE JOE and GREEN DAY

© 1997 WB MUSIC CORP. (ASCAP)
and GREEN DAZE MUSIC (ASCAP)
All Rights Administered by WB MUSIC CORP.
All Rights Reserved.

The song "Good Riddance (Time of Your Life)" was featured on Green Day's 1997 album *Nimrod*. The band has sold over 65 million records worldwide and has won Grammy Awards for both Best Rock Album and Record of the Year. The tune's lyrics are about life's challenges and turning points. Because it refers to having the "time of your life," it's often played at proms and graduations.

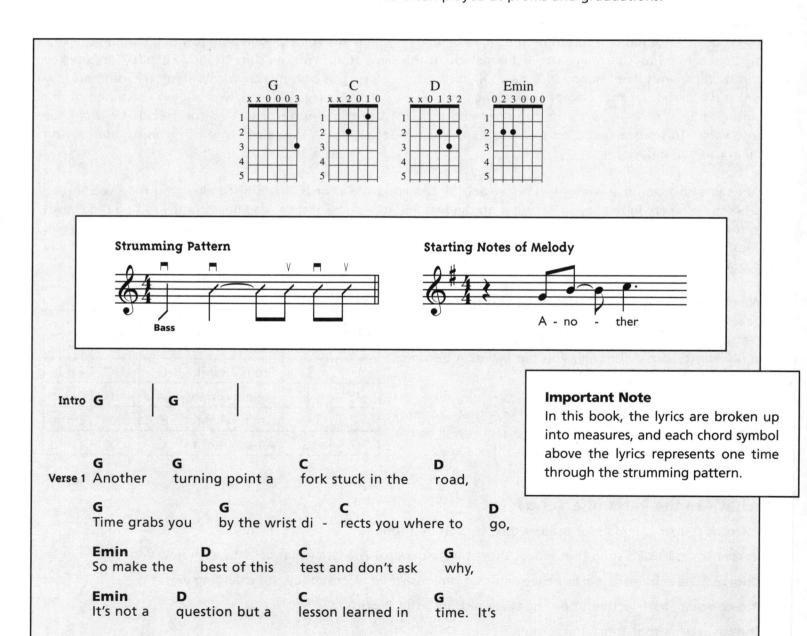

Important Note
In this book, the lyrics are broken up into measures, and each chord symbol above the lyrics represents one time through the strumming pattern.

Intro G | G |

Verse 1
G   G   C   D
Another   turning point a   fork stuck in the   road,

G   G   C   D
Time grabs you   by the wrist di -   rects you where to   go,

Emin   D   C   G
So make the   best of this   test and don't ask   why,

Emin   D   C   G
It's not a   question but a   lesson learned in   time. It's

Chorus

Emin	G	Emin	G
something unpre -	dictable but	in the end it's	right. I

Emin	D	G	G
hope you had the	time of your	life.	

Verse 2

G	G	C	D
So take the	photographs and	still frames in your	mind.

G	G	C	D
Hang it	on a shelf in	good health and good	time.

Emin	D	C	G
Tattoos and	memories and	dead skin on	trial.

Emin	D	C	G
For what it's	worth it was	worth all the	while. It's

Chorus

Emin	G	Emin	G
something unpre -	dictable but	in the end it's	right. I

Emin	D	G	G
hope you had the	time of your	life.	

*Since their major-label debut in 1994 (Dookie), **Green Day** has continued to show that they are masters of the 3- and 4-chord pop-punk rock song.*

Losing My Religion

Words and Music by WILLIAM BERRY, PETER BUCK, MICHAEL MILLS, and MICHAEL STIPE

R.E.M. guitarist Peter Buck wrote the music for "Losing My Religion" while practicing in front of the television. He had just purchased his first mandolin and was trying to figure out how to play it. He did something right—this became the band's biggest hit in the United States, climbing to number four on the Billboard Hot 100.

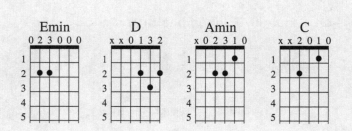

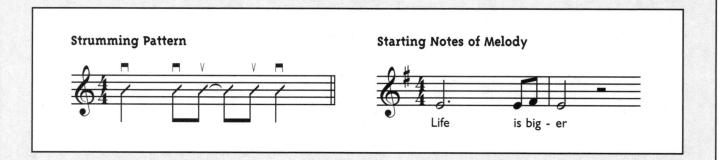

Strumming Pattern

Starting Notes of Melody

Life   is big - er

* Important Note
If a chord symbol is not aligned directly over a word of the lyrics, it means you should start singing *after* the first beat of that measure.

Intro   **Emin** | **Emin** |

         Emin   **Emin**   **D***   **D**
Verse 1   Life is   bigger,   it's bigger than   you, and you are

         Emin   **Emin**   **D**
not me; the   lengths that I will   go to, the

D   **Emin**   **Emin**
distance in your   eyes;

D   **D**   **Amin**   **Amin**
   oh no I've   said too   much,   I set it

D   **D**
up.   That's me in the

Verse 2

```
Emin        Emin              D
corner,     that's me in the   spotlight,

D                 Emin  Emin       D              D
losing my rel - igion,    trying to    keep up with   you, and I

Emin                    Emin  D
don't know if I can     do it,   oh no I've

D           Amin      Amin        D
said too    much, I    haven't said en - ough.    I
```

Chorus

```
D                          C          C
thought that I heard you    laughing; I    thought that I heard you

Emin  Emin   C              C          Emin  D
sing;    I    think I thought I    saw you    try.    Every
```

Verse 3

```
Emin        Emin          D
whisper of    every waking    hour. I'm

D                 Emin  Emin       D
Choosing my con - fessions    trying to    keep an eye on

D           Emin
you; like a    hurt lost and blinded

Emin  D           D              Amin  Amin      D    D
fool;    Oh no I've    said too    much,    I set it    up.    Consider
```

Verse 4

```
Emin        D                D
this, con - sider this the    hint of the centu - ry, consider

Emin        Emin       D              D
this, the    slip that    brought me to my    knees, failed,

Emin                Emin       D          D
What if all these    fantasies come    flailing a - round, now I've

Amin  Amin    D
said,    too    much. I
```

Chorus

```
D                          C
thought that I heard you    laughing, I

C                          Emin  Emin   C              C
thought that I heard you    sing;    I    think I thought I    saw you

Emin  Emin   C              C          Emin            D         Emin
try;    but    that was just a    dream, just a    dream, just a    dream, dream.
```

Wild Night

Words and Music by VAN MORRISON

Van Morrison wrote "Wild Night," as well as other classics like "Brown Eyed Girl" and "Into the Mystic." He was inducted into the Rock and Roll Hall of Fame in 1993 for his songwriting and unique blend of musical influences. Even though the song was written in 1971, "Wild Night" still remains popular because of its driving feel and party theme.

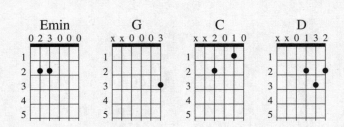

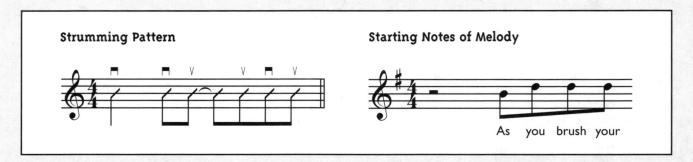

	Emin		Emin		Emin	
Intro					As you brush your	

	Emin	Emin	G	G
Verse 1	shoes and	stand before the	mirror;	and you comb your

	Emin	Emin	G	G
	hair,	grab your coat and	hat;	and you walk the

	Emin	Emin	G	Emin
	streets	tryin' to re - member	all the	

	C	D	G	G
	wild breezes	in your memory	of her.	And every-

	Emin		C	
Pre-Chorus	thing looks so com - plete		when you're	

	Emin	C	Emin
	walkin' out on the	street, and the	wind catches your

	C	D	D
	feet, and sends you	flyin'	cryin'

Chorus

Emin	C	D	Emin

Ooh - - - - - Ooh - wee!

Emin	D	G	G

Wild   night is   calling.   And all the

Verse 2

Emin	Emin	G	G

girls walk by,   dressed up for each   other,   and the

Emin	Emin	G	G

boys do the boogie-woogie   on the corner of the   street,   and all the

Emin	Emin	G	Emin

people passin' by just   stare in wild   wonder,   and the

C	D	G	G

inside juke-box   roars out just like   thunder.   And every-

Pre-Chorus

Emin	C

-thing looks so com - plete, when you're

Emin	C	Emin

walkin' out on the   street, and the   wind catches your

C	D	D

feet and sends you   flyin'   cryin'

Chorus

Emin	C	D	Emin

Ooh - - - - - Ooh - wee!

Emin	D	G	G

Wild   night is   calling.   The

Outro

Emin	Emin	G	G

wi - - - - ild night is   calling;   the

Emin	Emin	G	G

wi - - - - ild night is   calling;   Come on out and

Emin	Emin	G	G

dance;   come on out and   make romance;   Come on out and

Emin	D	G	G

dance,   make ro - mance.

Take It Easy

Words and Music by JACKSON BROWNE
and GLENN FREY

The Eagles' first album produced three Top 40 singles. The first single, "Take It Easy," is a song written by Glenn Frey and his neighbor and fellow country-folk rocker Jackson Browne. Frey heard Browne recording it, contributed two lines to it (for which he got co-writing credit), and asked if the Eagles could use it. Browne agreed, and the song reached number 12 on the Billboard Hot 100, propelling the Eagles to stardom.

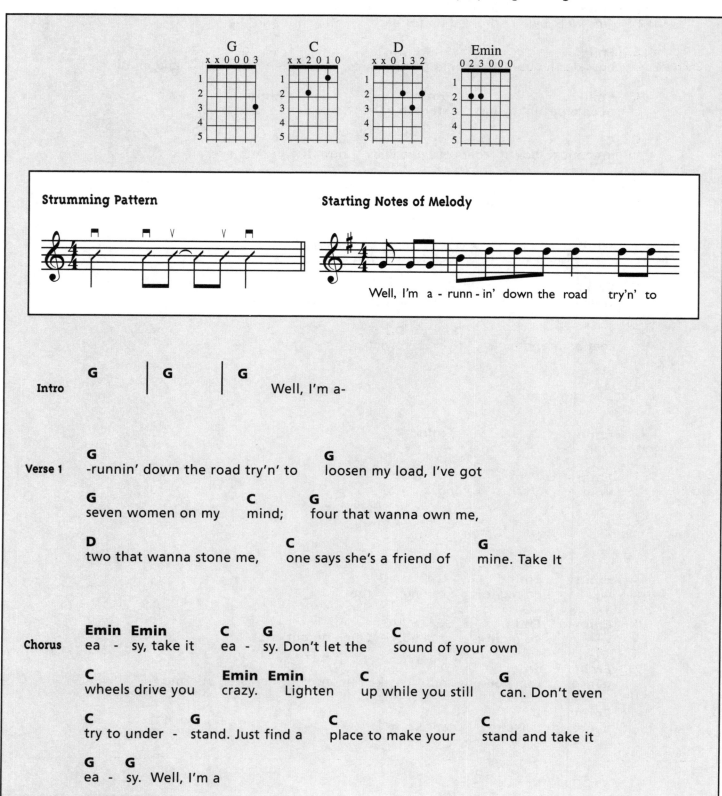

Intro

| G | G | G |

Well, I'm a-

Verse 1

G
-runnin' down the road try'n' to

G
loosen my load, I've got

G
seven women on my

C
mind;

G
four that wanna own me,

D
two that wanna stone me,

C
one says she's a friend of

G
mine. Take It

Chorus

Emin   Emin
ea - sy, take it

C   G
ea - sy. Don't let the

C
sound of your own

C
wheels drive you

Emin   Emin
crazy.   Lighten

C
up while you still

G
can. Don't even

C
try to under -

G
stand. Just find a

C
place to make your

C
stand and take it

G   G
ea - sy. Well, I'm a

Verse 2

G   G
standin' on a corner in   Winslow, Arizona, it's

G   C   G
such a fine sight to   see. It's a girl, my Lord, in a

D   C   G
flatbed Ford, slowin'   down to take a look at me. Come on,

Chorus

Emin Emin   C   G
ba - by, don't say may - be. I've gotta

C   C   Emin Emin
know if your sweet love is gonna save me. We may

C   G   C   G
lose and we may win, though we will never be here a - gain. So open

C   C   G G
up, I'm climbin' in, so take it eas - y. Well I'm a-

Verse 3

G   G
-runnin' down the road try'n' to loosen my load, got a

G   C   G
world of trouble on my mind. Lookin' for a lover who

D   C   G
won't blow my cover, she's so hard to find. Take it

Chorus

Emin Emin   C   G
eas - y, take it eas - y. Don't let the

C   C   Emin Emin
sound of your own wheels make you crazy. Come on,

C G   C G
ba - by, don't say may - be. I gotta

C   C   G G
know if your sweet love is gonna save me. Oh, we got it

G D C C   G D C C Emin
eas - - y. We oughta take it eas - - y.

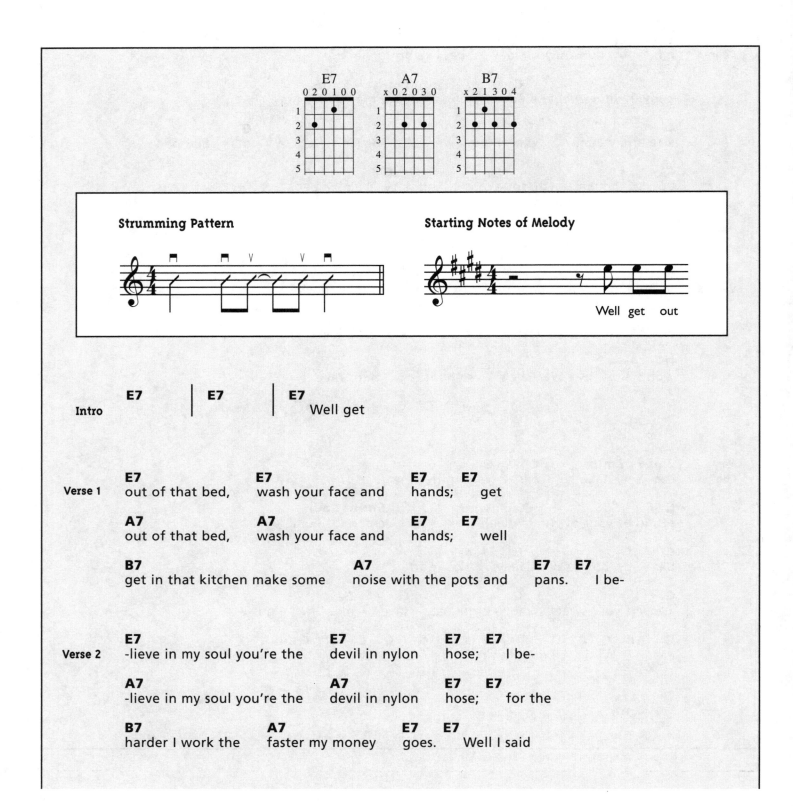

Shake, Rattle and Roll

Track 6

Words and Music by CHARLES E. CALHOUN

"Shake, Rattle and Roll" is a standard 12-bar blues song written by Jesse Stone under his pen name Charles E. Calhoun. It was originally written for Kansas City blues singer Big Joe Turner, whose recording became a number one R&B hit. However, the best-known version was recorded by Bill Haley & His Comets. The Bill Haley version is one of the most influential classics of early rock 'n' roll.

E7   A7   B7

Strumming Pattern

Starting Notes of Melody

Well get out

Intro

| E7 | E7 | E7 |

Well get

Verse 1

E7
out of that bed,   E7 wash your face and   E7   E7 hands;   get

A7
out of that bed,   A7 wash your face and   E7   E7 hands;   well

B7
get in that kitchen make some   A7 noise with the pots and   E7   E7 pans.   I be-

Verse 2

E7
-lieve in my soul you're the   E7 devil in nylon   E7   E7 hose;   I be-

A7
-lieve in my soul you're the   A7 devil in nylon   E7   E7 hose;   for the

B7
harder I work the   A7 faster my money   E7   E7 goes.   Well I said

Chorus

E7	E7	E7	E7
shake, rattle and	roll; I said	shake rattle and	roll; I said

A7	A7	E7	E7
shake, rattle and	roll; I said	shake rattle and	roll; well you

B7	A7	E7 E7	
won't do right to	save your doggone	soul. I'm like the	

Verse 3

E7	E7	E7 E7	
one-eyed cat	peeping in a seafood	store; I'm like the	

A7	A7	E7 E7	
one-eyed cat	peeping in a seafood	store; well I can	

B7	A7	E7 E7	
look at you tell you	ain't no child no	more. I be-	

Verse 4

E7	E7	E7 E7	
-lieve you're doing me	wrong and now I	know; I be-	

A7	A7	E7 E7	
-lieve you're doing me	wrong and now I	know; 'cause	

B7	A7	E7 E7	
harder I work the	faster my money	goes. Well I said	

Chorus

E7	E7	E7	E7
shake, rattle and	roll; I said	shake rattle and	roll; I said

A7	A7	E7	E7
shake, rattle and	roll; I said	shake rattle and	roll; well you

B7	A7	E7 E7	
won't do right to	save your doggone	soul. I went	

Verse 5

E7	E7	E7 E7	
over the hill,	way down under -	neath; I went	

A7	A7	E7 E7	
over the hill,	way down under -	neath; you make me	

B7	A7	E7 E7	
roll my eyes and	then you make me grit my	teeth. Well I said	

Chorus

E7	E7	E7	E7
shake, rattle and	roll; I said	shake rattle and	roll; I said

A7	A7	E7	E7
shake, rattle and	roll; I said	shake rattle and	roll; well you

B7	A7	E7 E7	
won't do right to	save your doggone	soul.	

Margaritaville

Words and Music by JIMMY BUFFETT

Jimmy Buffett wrote "Margaritaville" in 1977 while recuperating in Key West, Florida after a hectic tour. The song describes the singer's laid-back, tropical lifestyle. "Margaritaville" has become Buffett's theme song and the inspiration for his business enterprises such as the Margaritaville Cafe restaurant chain.

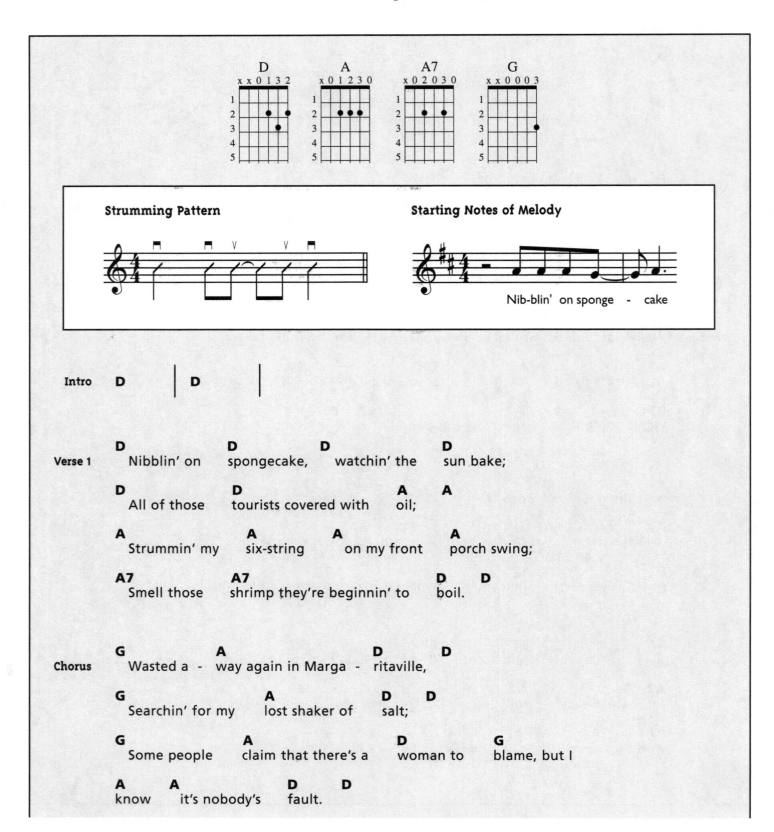

Intro	**D**	**D**		

Verse 1

D Nibblin' on **D** spongecake, **D** watchin' the **D** sun bake;

D All of those **D** tourists covered with **A** oil; **A**

A Strummin' my **A** six-string **A** on my front **A** porch swing;

A7 Smell those **A7** shrimp they're beginnin' to **D** boil. **D**

Chorus

G Wasted a - **A** way again in Marga - **D** ritaville, **D**

G Searchin' for my **A** lost shaker of **D** salt; **D**

G Some people **A** claim that there's a **D** woman to **G** blame, but I

A know **A** it's nobody's **D** fault. **D**

Verse 2

D		D		D		D
Don't know the		reason,		stayed here all		season,

D		D			A	A
With nothing to		show but this brand new tat -			too;	

A		A	A		A	
But it's a real		beauty,	a Mexican		cutie,	

A7		A7		D	D
how it got		here I haven't a		clue.	

Chorus

G		A		D	D
Wasted a -		way again in Marga -		ritaville,	

G		A		D	D
Searchin' for my		lost shaker of		salt;	

G		A		D		G
Some people		claim that there's a		woman to		blame, now I

A	A		D	D
think	hell, it could be my		fault.	

Verse 3

D		D		D		D
I blew out my		flip-flop,		stepped on a		pop-top,

D		D		A	A
Cut my		heel, had to cruise on back		home;	

A		A	A		A
But there's booze in the		blender,	and soon it will		render

A7		A7		D	D
That frozen con -		coction that helps me hang		on.	

Chorus

G		A		D	D
Wasted a -		way again in Marga -		ritaville,	

G		A		D	D
Searchin' for my		lost shaker of		salt;	

G		A		D		G
Some people		claim that there's a		woman to		blame, but I

A	A		D	D
know	it's my own damn		fault.	Yes, and

G		A		D		G
some people		claim that there's a		woman to		blame, and I

A	A		D	D
know	it's my own damn		fault.	

Scarborough Fair

Track 8

Traditional

During medieval times, the seaside town of Scarborough, England was the site of a large yearly fair. People gathered from all over to buy and sell goods and conduct business. The narrator of this song asks his former lover to perform a series of impossible tasks (in this arrangement, we include only one—making a shirt without a seam). If she completes these tasks, he will take her back. Countless artists, including Simon and Garfunkel, have performed their own versions of this traditional tune.

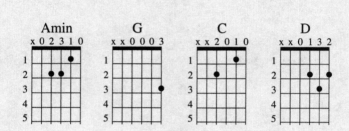

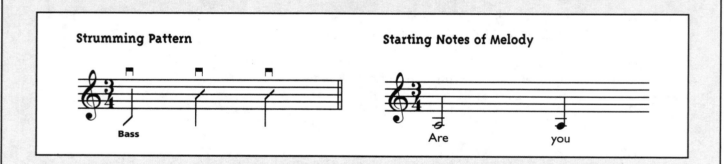

Intro | Amin | Amin | |

Verse 1

| Amin | Amin | G | Amin | C | Amin | D |
| Are you | going to | Scarborough | Fair? | Parsley, | sage, rose - | mary and |

| Amin | Amin | Amin | C | C | G | G |
| thyme; | re - | member | me to | one who lives | there, | for |

| Amin | G | G | Amin | Amin |
| once she | was a | true love of | mine. |

Verse 2

Amin   Amin   G   Amin C   Amin   D
Have her make me a cambric shirt; parsley, sage, rose - mary and

Amin Amin Amin C   C   G G
thyme; with - out no seam nor fine needle - work, and

Amin G   G   Amin Amin
then she'll be a true love of mine.

Verse 3

Amin   Amin   G   Amin C   Amin   D
If she tells me she can't, I'll re - ply; parsley, sage, rose - mary and

Amin Amin Amin C   C   G G
thyme; let me know that at least she will try, and

Amin G   G   Amin Amin
then she'll be a true love of mine.

Verse 4

Amin   Amin   G   Amin C   Amin   D
Love im - poses im - possible tasks; parsley, sage, rose - mary and

Amin Amin Amin C   C   G G
thyme; though not more than any heart asks, and

Amin G   G   Amin Amin
I must know she's a true love of mine.

Verse 1

Amin   Amin   G   Amin C   Amin   D
Dear, when thou has finished thy task; parsley, sage, rose - mary and

Amin Amin Amin C   C   G G
thyme; come to me, my hand for to ask, for

Amin G   G   Amin Amin
thou then art a true love of mine.

House of the Rising Sun

Traditional

The term "Rising Sun" was a popular name given to brothels in America from the 1800s into the 1920s. The original Rising Sun is believed to have been in the old French Quarter of New Orleans. The original melody of "House of the Rising Sun" finds its roots in 17th-century England, where it was a popular folk melody. The melody made its way into the Southern United States, and was a common tune for many early Southern musicians of both black and white descent. Many artists over the years have recorded their own versions of this traditional tune, including Woody Guthrie, Lead Belly, Bob Dylan, and the Animals.

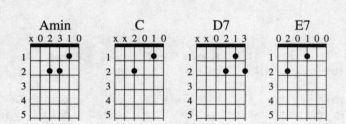

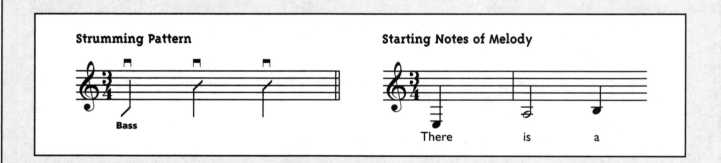

	Amin		Amin		Amin		
Intro						There	

	Amin	C	D7	D7	Amin	C	E7 E7
Verse 1	is a	house in	New Or -	leans, they	call the	Rising	Sun; It's

	Amin	C	D7	D7	Amin	E7	Amin E7
	been the	ruin of	many a poor	girl and	me, O	God, I'm	one. If

Verse 2

Amin	C		D7	D7	Amin	C		E7	E7
I had	listened to what		Mama	said, I'd	be at	home to -		day;	

Amin	C		D7	D7	Amin	E7		Amin	E7
Being so	young and		foolish,	let a	rambler	lead me a -		stray.	Go

Verse 3

Amin	C	D7	D7	Amin	C		E7	E7
tell my	baby	sister	never	do like	I have		done;	to

Amin	C	D7	D7	Amin	E7	Amin	E7
shun that	house in	New Or -	leans they	call the	Rising	Sun.	My

Verse 4

Amin	C	D7	D7	Amin	C		E7	E7
mother	she's a	tailor,	she	sewed these	new blue		jeans;	my

Amin	C	D7	D7	Amin	E7	Amin	E7
sweetheart,	he's a	drunkard,	he drinks	down in	New Or -	leans.	The

Verse 5

Amin	C	D7	D7	Amin	C		E7	E7
only	thing a	drunkard	needs is a	suitcase	and a		trunk;	the

Amin	C	D7	D7	Amin	E7	Amin	E7
only	time he's	satis - fied is	when he's	on a	drunk.		

Verse 6

Amin	C	D7	D7	Amin	C		E7	E7
Fills his	glasses	to the	brim,	passes	them ar -		ound;	

Amin	C	D7	D7	Amin	E7	Amin	E7
Only	pleasure he	gets out of	life is	roaming from	town to	town.	

Verse 7

Amin	C	D7	D7	Amin	C		E7	E7
One foot is	on the	platform	and the	other one	on the		train;	I'm

Amin	C	D7	D7	Amin	E7	Amin	E7
going	back to	New Or -	leans to	wear that	ball and	chain.	

Verse 8

Amin	C	D7	D7	Amin	C		E7	E7
Going	back to	New Or -	leans, my	race is	almost		run;	

Amin	C		D7	D7	Amin	E7	Amin	Amin
Going	back to spend the		rest of my	days be -	neath that	Rising	Sun.	

Sloop John B

Traditional

"Sloop John B" is a track on one of the most popular albums of all time, The Beach Boys' *Pet Sounds*. What many people don't know is the Beach Boys song was based on the traditional West Indies folk song shown here. The *John B.* was a sponge-diving boat whose crew had a reputation for drinking and partying. Perhaps because of its crew's bad habits, the ship sank sometime around 1900 in the Bahamas.

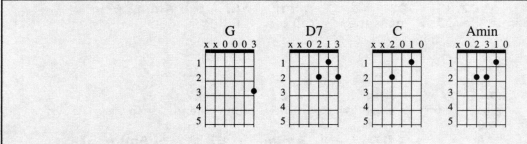

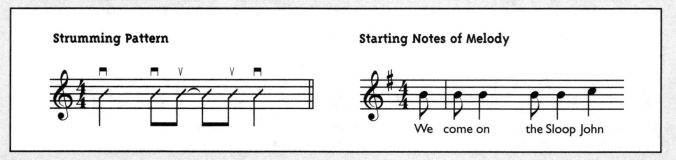

Intro
| G | G | G |
| | | We |

Verse 1

G .... G .... G .... G
come on the Sloop John ..... B, my ... grandfather and ..... me, a-

G .... G .... D7 .... D7 .... G
-round Nassau .. town we did .. roam, .. drinkin' all ..... night,

G .... C .... Amin ..... G .... D7 .... G .... G
Got into a ... fight, ... well, I ... feel so broke up, ... I want to go ... home.

Chorus

G .... G .... G .... G
Hoist up the John B's .. sails, .. see how the main sails .. set,

G .... G .... D7 .... D7
Call for the captain a - . shore, let me go .. home; ... let me go

G .... G .... C .... Amin
home, .. I want to go .... home, .. Well, I

G .... D7 .... G .... G
feel so broke up, .. I want to go ... home. .. Well the

Verse 2

G	G	G		G

first mate, he got   drunk,   broke up the captain's   trunk, the

G   **G**   **D7**   **D7**   **G**

Constable had to   come and take him a - way,   Sheriff John   Stone,

G   **C**   **Amin**

why don't you leave me a - lone? Yeah,   yeah well, I

G   **D7**   **G**

feel so break up,   I want to go   home.

Chorus

G   **G**   **G**   **G**

Hoist up the John B's   sails,   see how the main sails   set,

G   **G**   **D7**   **D7**

Call for the captain a - shore, let me go   home;   let me go

G   **G**   **C**   **Amin**

home,   I want to go   home,   Well, I

G   **D7**   **G**   **G**

feel so broke up,   I want to go   home.   Well the

Verse 3

G   **G**   **G**   **G**

poor cook he caught the   fits,   threw away all of my   grits,

G   **G**   **D7**   **D7**   **G**

Then he took and he   ate up all of my   corn,   let me go   home,

G   **C**   **Amin**   **G**   **D7**   **G**

I want to go   home,   this   is the worst trip   since I've been   born.

Chorus

G   **G**   **G**   **G**

Hoist up the John B's   sails,   see how the main sails   set,

G   **G**   **D7**   **D7**

Call for the captain a - shore, let me go   home;   let me go

G   **G**   **C**   **Amin**

home,   I want to go   home,   Well, I

G   **D7**   **G**   **G**

feel so broke up,   I want to go   home.

SECTION TWO: Holiday Songs

The number of different chords in a song has nothing to do with how popular or beautiful it is. Some of the most haunting and memorable holiday classics are very basic. Here are some more three- and four-chord songs to try.

Up on the Housetop

Words and Music by BENJAMIN HANBY

© 2008 ALFRED PUBLISHING CO., INC.
All Rights Reserved.

"Up on the Housetop" was composed by Benjamin Hanby in 1860. It was one of the first Christmas songs about Santa Claus instead of religious themes. In 2005, singer Kimberley Locke made music-industry history when her own recorded version of this traditional Christmas classic made the largest-ever leap into the Adult Contemporary Top 5.

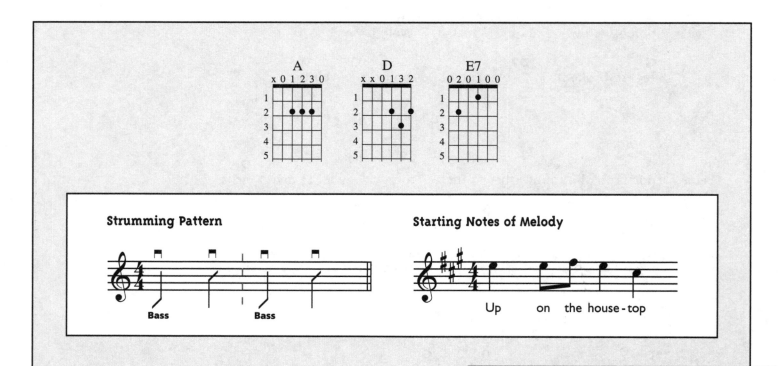

Intro	**A**	**A**

Verse 1	**A** Up on the housetop	**A** reindeer pause,
	D Out jumps good old	**E7** Santa Claus;
	A Down through the chimney with	**A** lots of toys,
	D **A** All for the little ones,	**E7** **A** Christmas joys.

Important Note

Several songs in this book have two chords in certain measures. (For example, see the last line on this page: "All for the little ones...") The dotted line in the strumming pattern above shows you how to divide the pattern between the two chords when there are two chords per measure. Listen to the CD to make sure you're getting this rhythm right.

Chorus

```
    D                A                    E7             A
    Ho, ho ho!    Who wouldn't go?    Ho, ho ho!    Who wouldn't go?

    A                         D
    Up on the housetop,    click, click, click,

    A                           E7         A
    Down through the chimney with    old Saint Nick.
```

Verse 2

```
    A                              A
    First comes the stocking of    little Nell,

    D              E7
    Oh, dear Santa    fill it well;

    A                      A
    Give her a dolly that    laughs and cries,

    D          A           E7       A
    One that will open and    shut her eyes.
```

Chorus

```
    D                A                    E7             A
    Ho, ho ho!    Who wouldn't go?    Ho, ho ho!    Who wouldn't go?

    A                         D
    Up on the housetop,    click, click, click,

    A                           E7         A
    Down through the chimney with    old Saint Nick.
```

Verse 3

```
    A                             A
    Next comes the stocking of    little Will,

    D                  E7
    Oh, just see what a    glorious fill;

    A                       A
    Here is a hammer and    lots of tacks,

    D    A          E7         A
    Also a ball and a    whip that cracks.
```

Chorus

```
    D                A                    E7             A
    Ho, ho ho!    Who wouldn't go?    Ho, ho ho!    Who wouldn't go?

    A                         D
    Up on the housetop,    click, click, click,

    A                           E7         A
    Down through the chimney with    old Saint Nick.
```

Joy to the World

Lyrics by ISAAC WATTS
Music by LOWELL MASON

The lyrics to "Joy to the World" started as a poem written by Isaac Watts in 1719. The poem was based on Psalm 98 of the Bible's Old Testament. American composer Lowell Mason set these words to music in 1839 and added a notation alluding to Handel as lyricist (it was common to attribute a song to Handel in those days in order to generate popularity). For over a century, the world believed that Handel had composed the song's lyrics. Eventually, musicologists discovered the truth, and credit was given to the rightful sources—Isaac Watts and the Biblical King David.

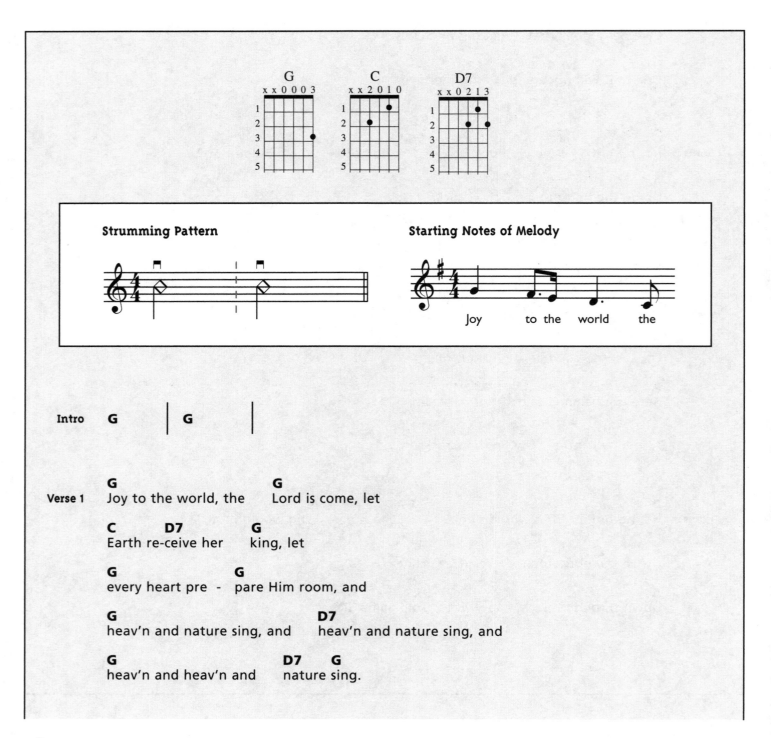

Intro   G | G |

Verse 1

G
Joy to the world, the
G
Lord is come, let

C   **D7**
Earth re-ceive her
G
king, let

G
every heart pre -
G
pare Him room, and

G
heav'n and nature sing, and
D7
heav'n and nature sing, and

G
heav'n and heav'n and
D7 **G**
nature sing.

Verse 2

G
Joy to the world, the

G
Savior reigns, let

C   D7
men their songs em -

G
ploy, while

G
fields and floods, rocks,

G
hills, and plains, re -

  G
- peat the sounding joy, re -

D7
peat the sounding joy, re -

  G
- peat, repeat the

D7   G
sounding joy.

Verse 3

G
He rules the world with

G
truth and grace, and

C   D7   G
makes the nations   prove, the

G
glories of his righteousness, and

G
wonders of His love, and

G
wonders of His love, and

D7
wonders of His love, and

G
wonders and wonders

D7 G
of His love.

Jingle Bells

Words and Music by JAMES PIERPOINT

Believe it or not, "Jingle Bells" was originally written for Thanksgiving! The author and composer of "Jingle Bells" was a minister named James Pierpont. He composed the song in 1857 for children celebrating Thanksgiving at his Boston Sunday school. The song was so popular that it was repeated at Christmas. "Jingle Bells," originally titled "One Horse Open Sleigh," is not only a holiday classic, but luckily for us, it's also easy to play!

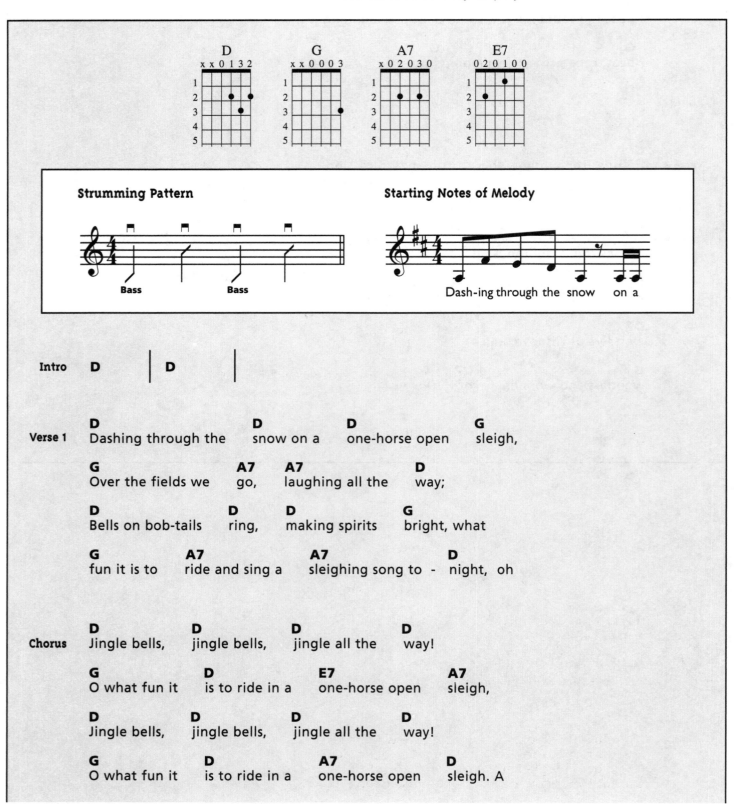

Intro   D | D |

Verse 1

D　　　　　　　　D　　　　D　　　　　　　G
Dashing through the 　snow on a 　one-horse open 　sleigh,

G　　　　　　　A7　　A7　　　　　　D
Over the fields we 　go, 　laughing all the 　way;

D　　　　　　　　D　　　D　　　　　　G
Bells on bob-tails 　ring, 　making spirits 　bright, what

G　　　　　A7　　　　　A7　　　　　　D
fun it is to 　ride and sing a 　sleighing song to - night, oh

Chorus

D　　　　　　D　　　　　D　　　　　　D
Jingle bells, 　jingle bells, 　jingle all the 　way!

G　　　　　　D　　　　　E7　　　　　　A7
O what fun it 　is to ride in a 　one-horse open 　sleigh,

D　　　　　　D　　　　　D　　　　　　D
Jingle bells, 　jingle bells, 　jingle all the 　way!

G　　　　　　D　　　　　A7　　　　　D
O what fun it 　is to ride in a 　one-horse open 　sleigh. A

Verse 2

D		D	D		G	
day or two a -	go, I	thought I'd take a	ride, and			

| G | | A7 | | A7 | | D | |
| soon Miss Fanny | Bright was | seated by my | side; the |

| D | | D | | D | | G | |
| horse was lean and | lank; Mis - | fortune seemed his | lot; he |

| G | | A7 | | A7 | | D | |
| got into a | drifted bank, and | we, we got up - | sot. |

Chorus

D		D		D		D	
Jingle bells,	jingle bells,	jingle all the	way!

| G | | D | | E7 | | A7 | |
| O what fun it | is to ride in a | one-horse open | sleigh, |

| D | | D | | D | | D | |
| Jingle bells, | jingle bells, | jingle all the | way! |

| G | | D | | A7 | | D | |
| O what fun it | is to ride in a | one-horse open | sleigh. A |

Verse 3

D		D	D		G	
day or two a -	go, the	story I must	tell, I

| G | | A7 | | A7 | | D | |
| went out on the | snow and | on my back I | fell; a |

| D | | D | | D | | G | |
| gent was riding | by, in a | one-horse open | sleigh, he |

| G | | A7 | | A7 | | D | |
| laughed as there I | sprawling lie, but | quickly drove a - | way. |

Chorus

Jingle bells, jingle bells, jingle all the way!
O what fun it is to ride in a one-horse open sleigh,
Jingle bells, jingle bells, jingle all the way!
O what fun it is to ride in a one-horse open sleigh.

Verse 4

D		D	D		G	
Now the ground is	white,	go it while you're	young,

| G | | A7 | | A7 | | D | |
| Take the girls to - | night and | sing this sleighing | song; just |

| D | | D | | D | | G | |
| get a bob-tailed | bay two - | forty as his | speed, |

| G | | A7 | | A7 | | D | |
| Hitch him to an | open sleigh and | crack! you'll take the | lead. |

Chorus

Jingle bells, jingle bells, jingle all the way!
O what fun it is to ride in a one-horse open sleigh,
Jingle bells, jingle bells jingle all the way!
O what fun it is to ride in a one-horse open sleigh.

Auld Lang Syne

Track 14

Lyrics by ROBERT BURNS

"Auld Lang Syne" is the unofficial theme song of New Year's Eve. Of Scottish origin, the words translate into "old long ago." The lyrics of this composition are often credited to Scottish poet Robert Burns; however, he actually adapted the words from ancient lore. The music's origin is unknown. Guy Lombardo and his band, The Royal Canadians, introduced "Auld Lang Syne" into our contemporary New Year's Eve tradition. Lombardo first played it for a 1929 radio broadcast, and we're still playing it today.

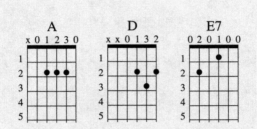

Strumming Pattern

Starting Notes of Melody

Should auld   ac-quaint-ance

Intro

| A | A | A | Should |

Verse 1

A	E7
auld acquaintance	be forgot, and

A	D
never brought to	mind? Should

A	E7
auld acquaintance	be forgot and the

D E7	A
days of auld lang	syne? And

A	E7
days of auld lang	syne, my dear, and

A	D
days of auld lang	syne, Should

A	E7
auld acquaintance	be forgot and

D E7	A
days of auld lang	syne? And

Verse 2

A   E7
here's a hand my   trusty friend, and

A   D
give a hand of   thine, we'll

A   E7
take a cup of   kindness yet for

D E7   A
auld lang   syne. For

A   E7
auld lang   syne, my dear, for

A   D
auld lang   syne, we'll

A   E7
take a cup of   kindness yet for

D E7   A
auld lang   syne.

Scottish Poet **Robert Burns** *(1759–1796).*

Silent Night

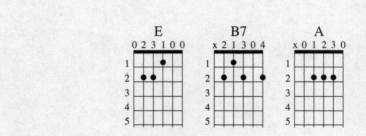

Lyrics by JOSEPH MOHR
Music by FRANZ X. GRUBER
English Translation by JOHN YOUNG

In 1818, when Christmas Eve was only hours away, Father Joseph Mohr's seasonal hymn was still incomplete due to a broken organ. He decided to use the lyrics from a poem he had written a few years before, with the title "Silent Night." He then turned to organist Franz Gruber for the music. With Father Joseph on the guitar and Franz Gruber singing the melody, that night made history. It was the first time the congregation had ever heard a guitar played in church, as well as the debut of one of our most popular Christmas songs.

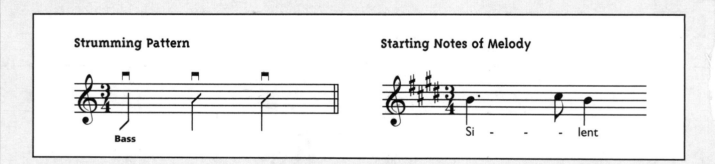

Intro E | E |

E	**E**	**E**	**E**	**B7**	**B7**	**E**	**E**
Silent	night,	holy	night,	all is	calm,	all is	bright;

A	**A**	**E**	**E**
Round yon	Virgin,	mother and	Child;

A	**A**	**E**	**E**
Holy	infant so	tender and	mild;

B7	**B7**	**E**	**E**	**E**	**B7**	**E** **E**
Sleep in	heavenly	pe- - -ace,		sleep in	heavenly	peace.

Verse 1

Verse 2

E	E	E	E	B7	B7	E	E
Silent	night,	holy	night,	shepherds	quake	at the	sight;

A	A	E	E
Glories	stream from	heaven a -	far;

A	A	E	E
Heavenly	hosts sing	Al-le-lu -	ia!

B7	B7	E	E	E	B7	E	E
Christ the	Saviour is	bo- -	-rn!	Christ the	Saviour is	born!	

Verse 3

E	E	E	E	B7	B7	E	E
Silent	night,	holy	night,	wondrous	star,	lend thy	light;

A	A	E	E
With the	angels	let us	sing

A	A	E	E
Alle -	luia	to our	King!

B7	B7	E	E	E	B7	E	E
Christ the	Saviour is	he- -	-re,	Jesus the	Saviour is	here!	

Verse 4

E	E	E	E	B7	B7	E	E
Silent	night,	holy	night,	Son of	God,	love's pure	light;

A	A	E	E
Radiant	beams from	Thy holy	face,

A	A	E	E
With the	dawn of re -	deeming	grace,

B7	B7	E	E	E	B7	E
Jesus	Lord at thy	bir- -	-th,	Jesus	Lord at thy	birth.

Deck the Hall

Track 16

Traditional

The music to "Deck the Hall" is an old Welsh melody. The "fa-la-la" refrains were probably originally played on the harp. The lyrics were added in 19th-century America when the country had a fascination with all things English, especially Charles Dickens' colorful writings. The lyrics help us to imagine the Christmas greens that were strung up inside England's wealthy estates.

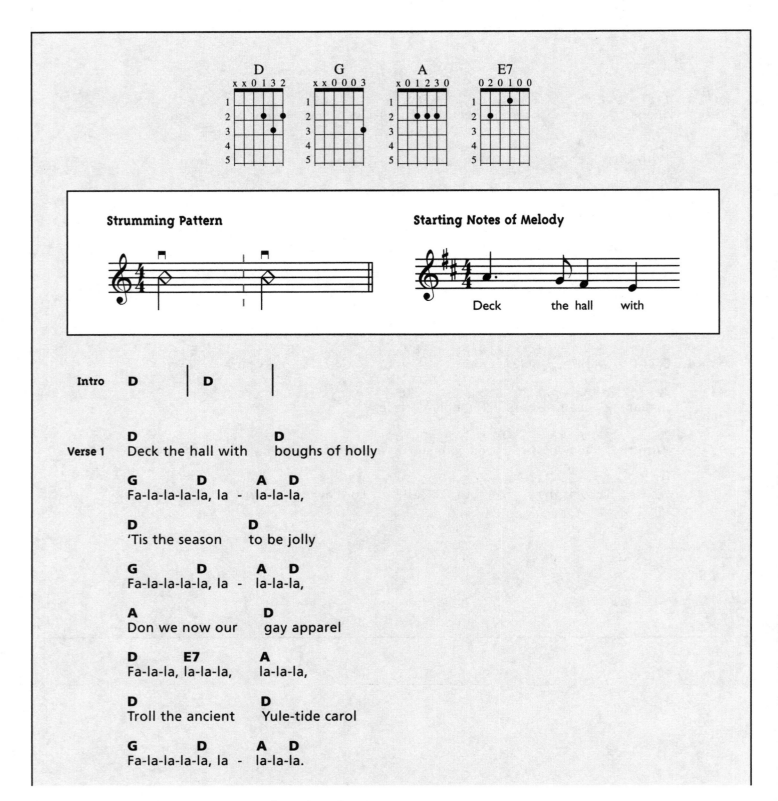

Intro   D | D |

Verse 1

D
Deck the hall with   **D** boughs of holly

G   **D**   **A**   **D**
Fa-la-la-la-la, la - la-la-la,

D   **D**
'Tis the season   to be jolly

G   **D**   **A**   **D**
Fa-la-la-la-la, la - la-la-la,

A   **D**
Don we now our   gay apparel

D   **E7**   **A**
Fa-la-la, la-la-la,   la-la-la,

D   **D**
Troll the ancient   Yule-tide carol

G   **D**   **A**   **D**
Fa-la-la-la-la, la - la-la-la.

Verse 2

   D   **D**
See the blazing   Yule before us

G   **D**   **A**   **D**
Fa-la-la-la-la, la - la-la-la,

D   **D**
Strike the harp and   join the chorus

G   **D**   **A**   **D**
Fa-la-la-la-la, la - la-la-la,

A   **D**
Follow me in   merry measure

D   **E7**   **A**
Fa-la-la, la-la-la,   la-la-la,

D   **D**
While I tell of   Yule-tide treasure

G   **D**   **A**   **D**
Fa-la-la-la-la, la - la-la-la.

Verse 3

   D   **D**
Fast away the   old year passes

G   **D**   **A**   **D**
Fa-la-la-la-la, la - la-la-la,

D   **D**
Hail the new year,   lads and lasses

G   **D**   **A**   **D**
Fa-la-la-la-la, la - la-la-la,

A   **D**
Sing we joyous,   all together

D   **E7**   **A**
Fa-la-la, la-la-la,   la-la-la,

D   **D**
Heedless of the   wind and weather

G   **D**   **A**   **D**
Fa-la-la-la-la, la - la-la-la.

All Through the Night

Traditional
English Lyrics by HAROLD BOULTON

"All Through the Night" was first published under the name "Ar Hyd y Nos" in *Musical Relicks of the Welsh Bards* (1784). The first English lyrics were possibly written by Amelia Opie and were sung to an English setting, "Here beneath a willow weepeth poor Mary Ann." Those lyrics were eventually replaced by Harold Boulton's now familiar lyrics.

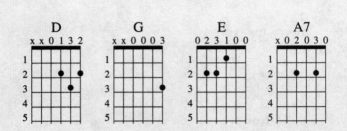

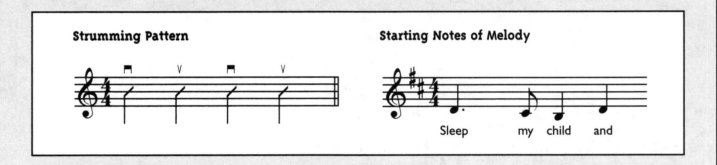

Intro D | D |

Verse 1

D   G   E   A7
Sleep my   child and   peace at - tend thee

G   A7   D   D
All   through the   night,

D   G   E   A7
Guardian   angels   God will   send thee

G   A7   D   D
All   through the   night,

G   G   G   G
Soft the   drowsy   hours are   creeping,

G   G   A7   A7
Hill and   vale in   slumber   sleeping,

D   G   E   A7
I my   loving   vigil   keeping,

G   A7   D   D
All   through the   night.

Verse 2

```
D              G              E              A7
While the      moon her       watch is       keeping

G     A7              D       D
All   through the     night,

D              G              E              A7
While the      weary          world is        sleeping

G     A7              D       D
All   through the     night,

G              G              G              G
O'er they      spirit         gently         stealing,

G              G              A7             A7
Visions        of de -        light re -     vealing,

D              G              E              A7
Breathes a     pure and       holy           feeling

G     A7              D       D
All   through the     night.
```

Verse 3

```
D              G              E              A7
Love, to       thee my        thoughts are   turning

G     A7              D       D
All   through the     night,

D              G              E              A7
All for        thee my        heart is       yearning

G     A7              D       D
All   through the     night,

G              G              G              G
Though sad     fate our       lives may      sever,

G              G              A7             A7
Parting        will not       last for -     ever,

D              G              E              A7
There's a      hope that      leaves me      never,

G     A7              D       D
All   through the     night.
```

Ma'oz Tzur (Rock of Ages)

Traditional Jewish Song

"Ma'oz Tzur" is a Hebrew song associated with the holiday of Hanukkah and its festival lights. The song dates back to at least the 13th century. Originally, it was sung only in the home, but in recent centuries has been used in the synagogue as well. "Ma'oz Tzur" has six stanzas (or verses), but only the first is well-known. This first verse is shown below, both in the original Hebrew and its literal English translation. On the next page is the popular, non-literal translation known in English as "Rock of Ages."

Verse 1
(Original Hebrew)

Ma'oz tzur y'shuati

L'kha na-eh l'shabei-ach

Tikon beyt t'filati

V'sham todah n'zabei-ach

L'eit tachin matbei-ach

Mitzar ha-m'nabei-ach

Az egmor b'shir mizmor

Chanukat ha-mizbei-ach

Az egmor b'shir mizmor

Chanukat ha-mizbei-ach

Verse 1
(Literal Translation)

Rocky Fortress of my Salvation

It is delightful to praise You

Restore my House of Prayer

And there we will give thanks with an offering

When you have prepared the slaughter

for the blaspheming foe

Then I will complete with a song of hymn

the dedication of the altar

Then I will complete with a song of hymn

the dedication of the altar

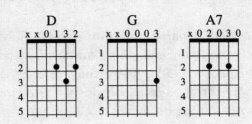

Strumming Pattern

Starting Notes of Melody

Rock of A - ges

Intro	**D**	**D**		

	D	**D**	**D**	**D**	**D**	**G**	**A7**	**D**
Verse 1	Rock of	Ages	let our	song,	praise thy	saving	pow -	er;

D	**D**	**D**	**D**	**D**	**G**	**A7** **D**
Thou a -	midst the	raging	foes,	wast our	shelt'ring	to - wer.

D	**D**	**D**	**D**	**D**	**D**	**A7** **A7**
Furious	they as -	sailed	us,	but Thine	arm a -	vailed us,

D	**D**	**A7**	**A7**	**D**	**G**
And Thy	word	broke their	sword,	when our	own strength

D	**D**	**D**	**D**	**A7**	**A7**
failed	us.	And Thy	word	broke their	sword,

D	**G**	**A7**	**D**
When our	own strength	failed	us.

SECTION THREE: Traditional/Campfire Songs

A song is usually considered a *traditional* tune when its copyright expires and it enters the public domain. Some of these songs were written well over a hundred years ago. Many are still being sung and recorded today. The tunes in this section will get you started, but there are thousands more traditional songs that you can play with only three or four chords. Because these songs are so beloved and well-known, they are great for many different occasions, including a friendly campfire.

Amazing Grace

Words and Music by JOHN NEWTON

John Newton wrote this hymn in Warwickshire, England after converting to Christianity. The lyrics "I once was lost, but now am found" describe the feeling Newton had after this experience. Before his conversion, Newton was the commander of a slave ship, and this experience is also woven into the lyrics.

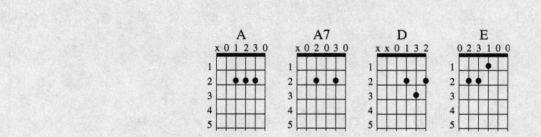

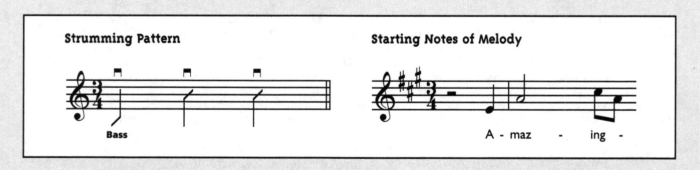

Intro

A	A	A
		A -

Verse 1

A	A7	D	A	A	A	E	E
- mazing	Grace, how	sweet the	sound, that	saved a	wretch like	me;	I

A	A7	D	A	A	E	D	A
once was	lost but	now I'm	found, was	blind but	now I	see.	'Twas

Verse 2

A	A7	D	A	A	A	E	E
Grace that	taught my	heart to	fear, and	Grace my	fears re -	lived;	how

A	A7	D	A	A	E	D	A
precious	did that	Grace ap -	pear the	hours I	first be -	lieved.	Through

Verse 3

A	A7	D	A	A	A	E	E
many	dangers,	toils and	snares, we	have al -	ready	come.	'Twas

A	A7	D	A	A	E	D	A
Grace that	brought us	safe thus	far, and	Grace will	lead us	home.	The

Verse 4

A	A7	D	A	A	A	E	E
Lord has	promised	good to	me, His	word my	hope se -	cures.	He

A	A7	D	A	A	E	D	A
will my	shield and	portion	be, as	long as	life en -	dures.	When

Verse 5

A	A7	D	A	A	A	E	E
we've been	here ten	thousand	years, bright	shining	as the	sun.	We've

A	A7	D	A	A	E	D	A
no less	days to	sing God's	praise then	when we've	first be -	gun.	A -

Repeat Verse 1

A	A7	D	A	A	A	E	E
- mazing	Grace how	sweet the	sound, that	saved a	wretch like	me,	I

A	A7	D	A	A	E	D	A
once was	lost but	now I'm	found, was	blind but	now I	see.	

The Water Is Wide

Traditional

"The Water Is Wide" (also known by its Scottish title "O Waly, Waly") is a folk song that dates back to the 1600s. Versions of this traditional tune have been recorded by James Taylor and a host of other popular artists.

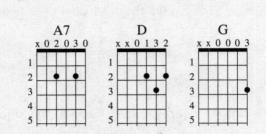

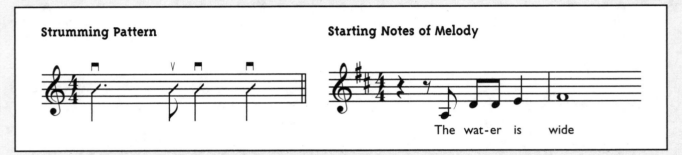

Strumming Pattern

Starting Notes of Melody

The wat-er is wide

Intro	**A7**		**A7**		

Verse 1

A7   **D**   **G**   **D**
The water is   wide,   I can't get   o'er,

D   **D**   **G**   **A7**
And neither   have   I wings to   fly;

A7   **D**   **G**   **D**
Give me a   boat   that will carry   two,

G   **D**   **A7**   **D**
And both shall   row   my love and   I.

Verse 2

A7   **D**   **G**   **D**
O love is   handsome,   and love is   fine,

D   **D**   **G**   **A7**
And love's a   jewel   when it's first   new;

A7   **D**   **G**   **D**
But love grows   old   and waxes   cold,

G   **D**   **A7**   **D**
And fades a - way   like morning   dew.

Verse 3
There is a ship, it's sailing the sea,
It's loaded deep as deep can be,
But not so deep as my love for him,
I know not if I sink or swim.

Verse 4
The water is wide, I can't get o'er,
And neither have I wings to fly;
Give me a boat that will carry two,
And both shall row my love and I.

Bill Bailey

Words and Music by HUGHIE CANNON

"Bill Bailey," originally titled "Bill Bailey, Won't You Please Come Home" was written by Hughie Cannon (1877–1912) and published in 1902. It is a standard tune in the Dixieland and traditional jazz band repertoire. Most performers these days omit the verses and only sing the chorus section written below.

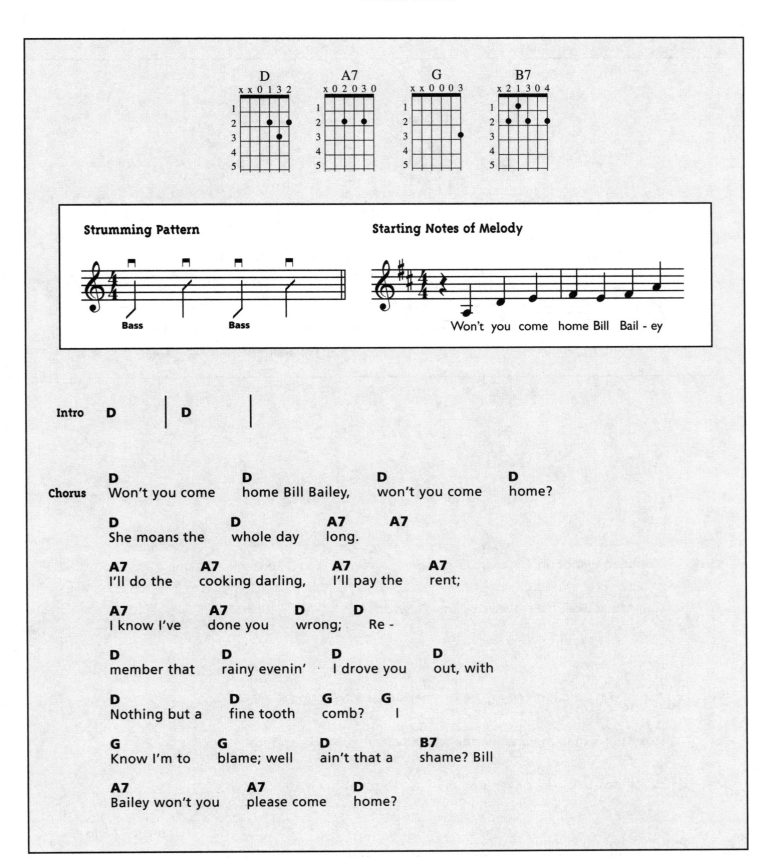

Intro   D | D |

Chorus

D		D		D		D	
Won't you come		home Bill Bailey,		won't you come		home?	

D		D		A7		A7	
She moans the		whole day		long.			

A7		A7		A7		A7	
I'll do the		cooking darling,		I'll pay the		rent;	

A7		A7		D		D	
I know I've		done you		wrong;		Re -	

D		D		D		D	
member that		rainy evenin'		I drove you		out, with	

D		D		G		G	
Nothing but a		fine tooth		comb?		I	

G		G		D		B7	
Know I'm to		blame; well		ain't that a		shame? Bill	

A7		A7		D	
Bailey won't you		please come		home?	

 **Wandering**

Traditional

Singer-songwriter James Taylor is of Scottish descent and keeps ties to his ancestors through his music. Although he writes most of his own music, he has covered several Scottish folk ballads, including "Wandering." The traditional version of this song is printed here.

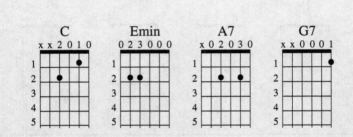

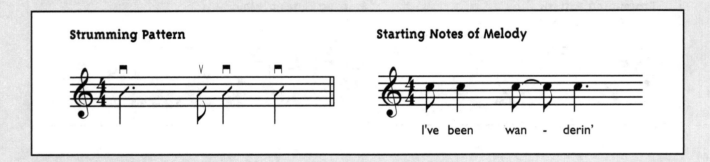

Intro C | C | |

Verse 1

C   **Emin**   **A7**   **G7**
I've been wanderin'   early late, from   New York City to the   Golden Gate, and it

C   **G7**   **C**   **C**
don't look like   I'll ever stop my   wanderin'.   My

Verse 2

C   **Emin**
daddy was an engineer, my   brother drives a hack, my

A7   **G7**
sister takes in laundry while the   baby balls the jack, and it

C   **G7**   **C**   **C**
don't look like   I'll ever stop my   wanderin'.   I've

Verse 3

C
been in the army, I've

Emin
worked on a farm, and

A7
all I've got to show is the

G7
muscle in my arm, and it

C
don't look like

G7
I'll ever stop my

C
wanderin'.

C
My

Verse 4

C
ma she died when

Emin
I was young, my

A7
daddy took to stealin' and

G7
he got hung and it

C
don't look like

G7
I'll ever stop my

C
wanderin'.

C

Verse 5

C
Snakes in the ocean,

Emin
eels in the sea, I let a

A7
redheaded woman make a

G7
fool out of me, and it

C
don't look like

G7
I'll ever stop my

C
wanderin'.

C

Verse 6

C
I've been wanderin'

Emin
early late, from

A7
New York City to the

G7
Golden Gate and it

C
don't look like

G7
I'll ever stop my

C
wanderin.

C
No it

C
don't look like

G7
I'll ever stop my

C
wanderin'.

Traditional

"Aura Lee" is a musical ode to a beautiful woman. The song dates back to the Civil War era. Elvis Presley borrowed the melody of "Aura Lee" for two of his songs: "Violet (Flower of N.Y.U.)," from the film *The Trouble with Girls* (1969), and his signature ballad "Love Me Tender" (1956).

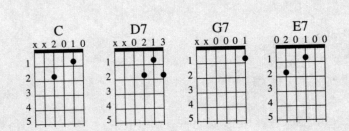

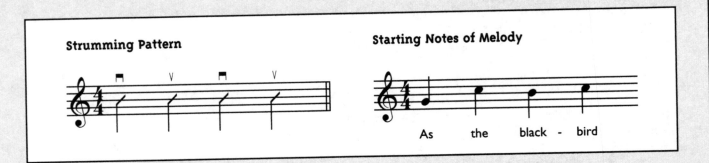

Intro   C | C |

Verse 1

C	D7	G7	C
As the blackbird	in the spring,	'neath the willow	tree,

C	D7	G7	C
Sat and piped, I	heard him sing,	sing of Aura	Lee.

Chorus

C	E7	C	E7
Aura Lee,	Aura Lee,	maid with golden	hair;

C	D7	G7	C
Sunshine came a -	long with thee, and	swallows in the	air.

Verse 2

C	D7	G7	C
In thy blush the	rose was born,	music when you	spoke,

C	D7	G7	C
Through thine azure	eyes, the morn,	sparkling seemed to	break.

Chorus

C	E7	C	E7
Aura Lee,	Aura Lee,	birds of crimson	wing,

C	D7	G7	C
Never song have	sung to me,	in that night, sweet	spring.

Verse 3

C	D7	G7	C
Aura Lee! The	bird may flee, the	willow's golden	hair,

C	D7	G7	C
Swing through winter	fitfully,	on the stormy	air.

Verse 4

C	D7	G7	C
Yet if thy blue	eyes I see,	gloom will soon de -	part;

C	D7	G7	C
For to me, sweet	Aura Lee is	sunshine through the	heart.

Verse 5

C	D7	G7	C
When the mistle -	toe was green,	'midst the winter's	snows,

C	D7	G7	C
Sunshine in thy	face was seen,	kissing lips of	rose.

Chorus

C	E7	C	E7
Aura Lee,	Aura Lee,	take my golden	ring;

C	D7	G7	C
Love and light re -	turn with thee, and	swallows with the	spring.

 **Rock of Ages**

Traditional Hymn

"Rock of Ages" is a popular Christian hymn. The words were written by Reverend Augustus Montague Toplady in 1763 and first published in *The Gospel Magazine* in 1775. The words have been set to a few different melodies through the years. The music we are most familiar with today was added around 1830. This song should not be confused with the Jewish hymn "Ma'oz Tzur" (page 38).

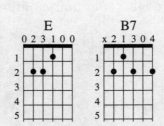

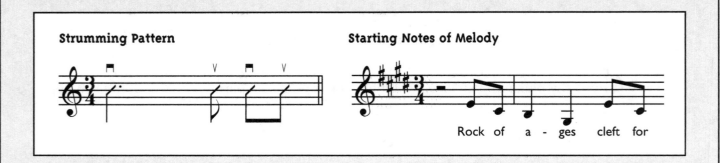

Strumming Pattern

Starting Notes of Melody

Rock of a - ges cleft for

Intro

E	E	E
		Rock of

Verse 1

E	**E**	**B7**	**E**
Ages, cleft for	me, let me	hide myself in	Thee; let the

B7	**E**	**B7**	**E**
water and the	blood, from Thy	riven side which	flowed, be of

E	**E**	**B7**	**E**
sin the double	cure; save from	wrath and make me	pure. Not the

Verse 2

E	E	B7	E
labour of my	hands can ful -	fil Thy law's de -	mands; could my

B7	E	B7	E
zeal no respite	know, could my	tears forever	flow, all for

E	E	B7	E
sin could not a -	tone; Thou must	save, and Thou a -	lone. Nothing

Verse 3

E	E	B7	E
in my hand I	bring, simply	to the cross I	cling; naked,

B7	E	B7	E
come to Thee for	dress; helpless,	look to Thee for	grace; foul, I

E	E	B7	E
to the fountain	fly; wash me,	Saviour, else I	die. While I

Verse 4

E	E	B7
draw this fleeting	breath, when my	eyelids close in

E	B7	E	B7
death, when I	soar to worlds un -	known, see Thee	on Thy judgement

E	E	E	B7	E
throne, Rock of	Ages, cleft for	me, let me	hide myself in	Thee.

Oh! Susanna

Lyrics and Music by STEPHEN FOSTER

Stephen Collins Foster (1826–1864) is sometimes referred to as the "father of American music." He wrote many well-known songs, including "Camptown Races," "Beautiful Dreamer," "Old Black Joe," "My Old Kentucky Home," and "Old Folks at Home (Swanee River)." One of his best-known songs is "Oh! Susanna," which you are about to learn.

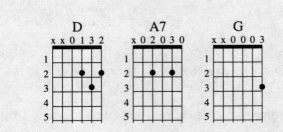

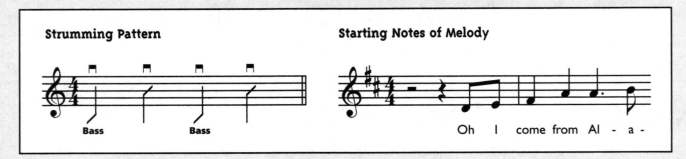

Intro

D	D	D	Oh I

Verse 1

D	D	D	A7
come from Ala -	bama with a	banjo on my	knee, I'm

D	D	A7	D
going to Louisi -	ana, my	true love for to	see. It

D	D	D	A7
rained all night the	day I left, the	weather it was	dry. The

D	D	A7	D
sun so hot I	froze to death; Su -	sanna, don't you	cry.

Chorus

G	G	D	A7
Oh, Su - sanna,	don't you cry for	me. For I

D	D	A7	D
come from Ala -	bama, with my	banjo on my	knee. I

Verse 2

D	D	D	A7
had a dream the	other night when	everything was	still, I

D	D	A7	D
thought I saw Su -	sanna	coming up the	hill, the

D	D	D
buckwheat cake was	in her mouth, the	tear was in her

A7	D	D	A7	D
eye, I said I'm	coming from	Dixieland, Su -	sanna don't you	cry.

Chorus

G	G	D	A7
Oh, Su - sanna,	don't you cry for	me. For I

D	D	A7	D
come from Ala -	bama, with my	banjo on my	knee. I

Verse 3

D	D
soon will be in	New Orleans and

D	A7	D	D
then I'll look a -	round, and	when I find my	gal Susanne, I'll

A7	D
fall upon the	ground.

Chorus

G	G	D	A7
Oh, Su - sanna,	don't you cry for	me. For I

D	D	A7	D
come from Ala -	bama, with my	banjo on my	knee.

Home on the Range

Lyrics by DR. BREWSTER M. HIGLEY
Music by DANIEL E. KELLY

Dr. Brewster M. Higley originally wrote the words to "Home on the Range" in the 1870s. It is based on his poem "My Western Home." The music was written by Daniel E. Kelley, a friend of Higley's. The lyrics have evolved through the years as the song was spread across the nation by settlers and cowboys. "Home on the Range" was adopted as the official state song of Kansas in 1947, and has become a sort of "national anthem" for the American West.

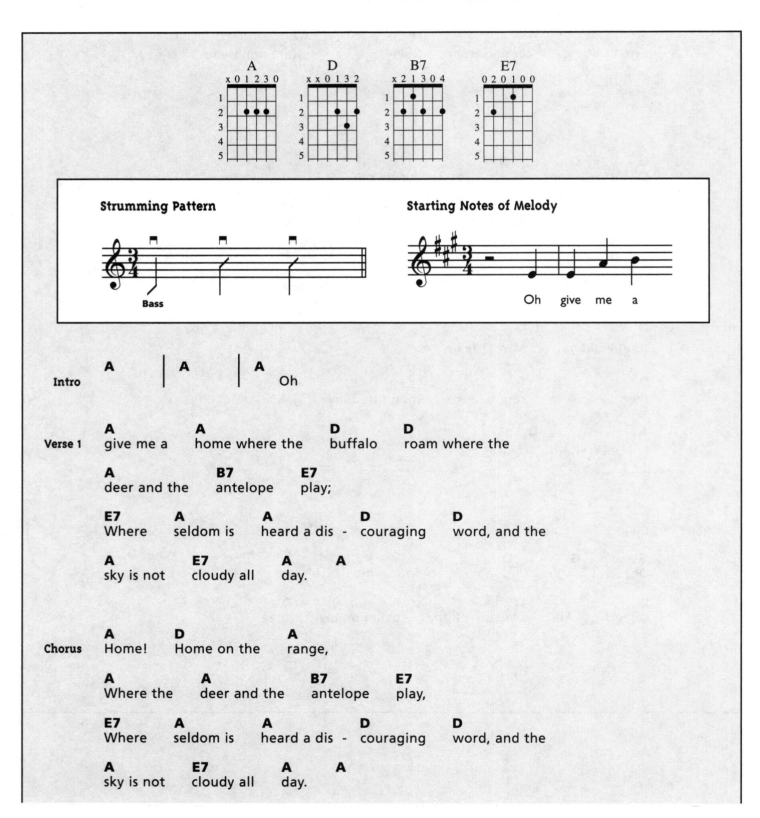

Intro
| A | A | A |
Oh

Verse 1
A — give me a   A — home where the   D — buffalo   D — roam where the
A — deer and the   B7 — antelope   E7 — play;
E7 — Where   A — seldom is   A — heard a dis -   D — couraging   D — word, and the
A — sky is not   E7 — cloudy all   A — day.   A

Chorus
A — Home!   D — Home on the   A — range,
A — Where the   A — deer and the   B7 — antelope   E7 — play,
E7 — Where   A — seldom is   A — heard a dis -   D — couraging   D — word, and the
A — sky is not   E7 — cloudy all   A — day.   A

Verse 2

A	A	A	D	D
Oh!	give me a	land where the	bright diamond	sand throws its

A	B7	E7	E7	A
light from the	glittering	streams,	Where	glideth a-

A	D	D	A	E7	A	A
long the	graceful white	swan, like the	maid in her	heavenly	dreams.	

Chorus

A	D	A
Home!	Home on the	range,

A	A	B7	E7
Where the	deer and the	antelope	play,

E7	A	A	D	D
Where	seldom is	heard a dis -	couraging	word, and the

A	E7	A
sky is not	cloudy all	day.

Verse 3

A	A	A	D	D
Oh!	give me a	gale of the	Solomon	vale, where the

A	B7	E7	E7	A
life streams with	buoyancy	flow;	On the	banks of the

A	D	D	A	E7	A	A
Beaver, where	seldom if	ever, any	poisonous	herbage doth	grow.	

Chorus

Home! Home on the range
Where the deer and the antelope play,
Where seldom is heard a discouraging word, and the
sky is not cloudy all day.

Verse 4

How often at night, when the heavens were bright, with the
light of the twinkling stars, have I stood here amazed, and
asked as I gazed, If their glory exceeds that of ours.

Chorus

Home! Home on the range
Where the deer and the antelope play,
Where seldom is heard a discouraging word, and the
sky is not cloudy all day.

Verse 5

I love the wild flowers in this bright land of ours, I
love the wild curlew's shrill scream; The
bluffs and white rocks, and antelope flocks that
graze on the mountains so green.

Chorus

Home! Home on the range
Where the deer and the antelope play,
Where seldom is heard a discouraging word, and the
sky is not cloudy all day.

Oh When the Saints Go Marching In

Traditional

"Oh When the Saints Go Marching In" was originally written as a spiritual gospel hymn, but was also used as traditional New Orleans "jazz funeral" music. On the way to the cemetery, the band would play a slow and mournful version of the tune, but after the burial, the band switched to the upbeat "Dixieland" style. While the tune is still heard as a slow spiritual number on rare occasions, it is more common to hear it played in a jazz style.

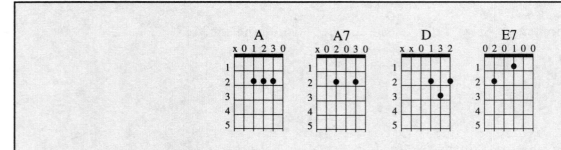

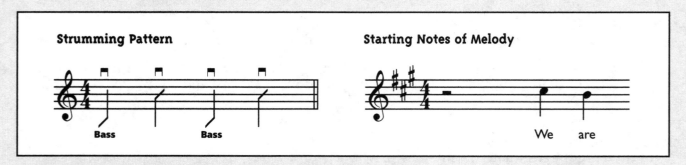

Intro	A	A	A We are

Verse 1

A	A7	D	D	A	A	E7
trav'ling	in the	footsteps,	of	those who've	gone be -	fore,

E7	A	A7 D	D	A	E7	A
and we'll	all be	reu - nited,	on a	new and	sunlit	shore.

Chorus

A	A	A	A A	A
Oh, when the	saints	go marching	in, Oh when the	saints go

A	E7 E7	A	A7	D
marching	in, Lord, how I	want to	be in that	number,

D	A	E7	A
when the	saints go	marching	in.

Verse 2

A		A	A		A	
And when the		sun	refuse to		shine,	

A		A	A		E7
And when the		sun re -	fuse to		shine,

E7		A	A7		D
Lord, how I		want to	be in that		number,

D		A	E7	A
When the		sun re -	fuse to	shine.

Verse 3

A		A	A		A
And when the		moon	turns red with		blood,

A		A	A		E7
And when the		moon turns	red with		blood,

E7		A	A7		D
Lord, how I		want to	be in that		number,

D		A	E7	A
When the		moon turns	red with	blood.

Verse 4

A		A	A		A
Oh, when the		trum -	pet sounds its		call,

A		A	A		E7
Oh, when the		trumpet	sounds its		call,

E7		A	A7		D
Lord, how I		want to	be in that		number,

D		A	E7	A
When the		trumpet	sounds its	call.

Verse 5

A	A	A7	D
Some	say this	world of	trouble,

D	A	A	E7
Is the	only	one we	need,

E7	A	A7	D
But I'm	waiting	for that	morning,

D	A	E7	A
When the	new world	is re -	vealed.

I've Been Working on the Railroad

Traditional

"I've Been Working on the Railroad" is a classic American folk tune. The first published version appeared in a book of Princeton University songs in 1894, under the title "Levee Song." Victor Records released the earliest known recording in 1927. The 1894 version includes a verse very much like the modern song, though in a different dialect and with lyrics that are controversial by today's standards.

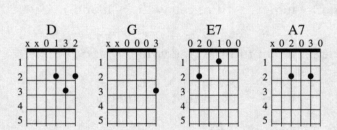

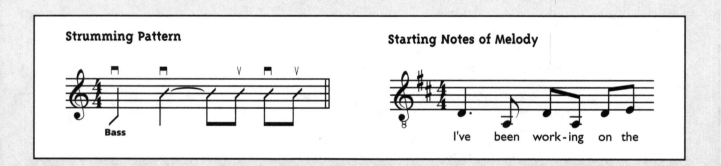

Intro D | D |

Verse 1

D
I've been working on the

D   G
railroad   all the live-long

D
day.

D
I've been working on the

D
railroad just to

E7
pass the time a -

A7
way.

A7
Don't you hear the whistle

D
blowing,

G
rise up so early in the

D
morn;

G
Don't you hear the captain

D
shouting,

A7
"Dinah, blow your

D
horn!"

Chorus

D
Dinah, won't you blow, **G** Dinah, won't you blow,

A7
Dinah, won't you blow your **D** horn?

D
Dinah, won't you blow, **G** Dinah, won't you blow,

A7
Dinah, won't you blow your **D** horn?

Verse 2

D
Someone's in the kitchen with **D** Dinah,

D
Someone's in the kitchen I **A7** know;

D
Someone's in the kitchen with **G** Dinah,

A7
Strummin' on the old ban - **D** jo! Singin'

Verse 3

D **D** **D** **A7**
Fi, fie, fiddly-i-o fi, fie, fiddly-i- o-o-o-o

D **G** **A7** **D**
Fi, fie, fiddly-i-o, strummin' on the old ban - jo.

Verse 4

D **D** **D** **A7**
Someone's makin' love to Dinah, someone's making love I know.

D **G** **A7** **D**
Someone's making love to Dinah, 'cause I can't hear the old ban- jo.

 **Tom Dooley**

Traditional

"Tom Dooley" is one of those easy songs that every acoustic guitarist plays when they're starting out. The Kingston Trio's version, recorded in 1958, is probably the best-known. The lyrics tell a morbid story; the old folk song is based on the 1866 murder of a girl named Laura Foster in North Carolina. Following is the traditional version of "Tom Dooley."

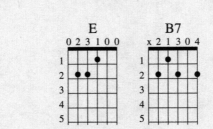

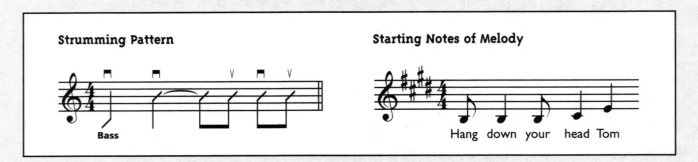

Intro	**E**	**E**		

	E	**E**	**E**	**B7**
Chorus	Hang down your head, Tom	Dooley,	Hang down your head and	cry,
	B7	**B7**	**B7**	**E**
	Hang down your head, Tom	Dooley,	Poor boy, you're bound to	die.

	E	**E**	**E**	**B7**
Verse 1	Met her on the	mountain,	there I took her	life,
	B7	**B7**	**B7**	**E**
	Met her on the	mountain,	stabbed her with my	knife.

Chorus

E		E	E		B7
Hang down your head, Tom		Dooley,	Hang down your head and		cry,

B7		B7	B7		E
Hang down your head, Tom		Dooley,	poor boy, you're bound to		die.

Verse 2

E	E	E		B7
This time to - morrow,	reckon where I'll	be,		

B7	B7	B7	E
Hadn't a-been for	Grayson, I'd a - been in Tennes - see.		

Chorus

E	E	E	B7
Hang down your head, Tom	Dooley,	hang down your head and	cry,

B7	B7	B7	E
Hang down your head, Tom	Dooley,	poor boy, you're bound to	die.

Verse 3

E	E	E	B7
This time to - morrow,	reckon where I'll	be,	

B7	B7	B7	E
Down in some lonesome	valley,	hangin' from a white oak	tree.

Chorus

E	E	E	B7
Hang down your head, Tom	Dooley,	hang down your head and	cry,

B7	B7	B7	E
Hang down your head, Tom	Dooley,	Poor boy, you're bound to	die.

Down in the Valley

Track 30

Traditional

Like many American folk songs, "Down in the Valley" was written in the 19th century. Because it was written so long ago, there are now many variations in the lyrics and number of verses. Most of the newer versions were simplified for school songbooks. The verses below seem to be the most common.

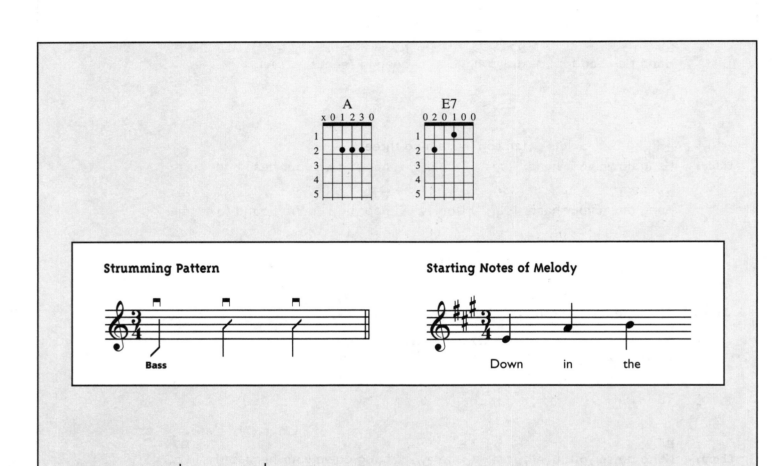

Intro   A | A |

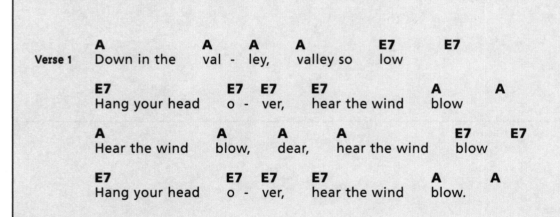

A		**A**	**A**	**A**	**E7**	**E7**
Verse 1 Down in the		val -	ley,	valley so	low	

E7		**E7**	**E7**	**E7**	**A**	**A**
Hang your head		o -	ver,	hear the wind	blow	

A		**A**	**A**	**A**	**E7**	**E7**
Hear the wind		blow,	dear,	hear the wind	blow	

E7		**E7**	**E7**	**E7**	**A**	**A**
Hang your head		o -	ver,	hear the wind	blow.	

Verse 2

A	A	A	A	E7	E7
Roses love	sun - shine,	violets love	dew		

E7	E7	E7	E7	A	A
Angels in	heav - en	know I love	you		

A	A	A	A	E7	E7
Know I love	you,	dear,	know I love	you	

E7	E7	E7	E7	A	A
Angels in	heav - en,	know I love	you.		

Verse 3

A	A	A	A	E7
Writing this	let - ter, con -	taining three	lines	

E7	E7	E7	E7	A	A
Answer my	ques - tion,	"Will you be	mine?"		

A	A	A	A	E7	E7
"Will you be	mine,	dear,	will you be	mine?"	

E7	E7	E7	E7	A	A
Answer my	ques - tion,	"Will you be	mine?"		

Verse 4

A	A	A	A	E7	E7
Down in the	val - ley,	valley so	low		

E7	E7	E7	E7	A	A
Hang your head	o - ver,	hear the wind	blow		

A	A	A	A	E7	E7
Hear the wind	blow,	dear,	hear the wind	blow	

E7	E7	E7	E7	A	A
Hang your head	o - ver,	hear the wind	blow.		

Down by the Riverside

Traditional

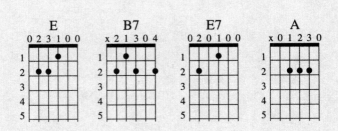

Many early American folk songs were originally spirituals sung by African-American slaves. "Down by the Riverside" and "We Shall Overcome" are just two of these songs that are still sung today. These are songs about struggle and hardship, but they are also full of hope. The music served as a mental escape for workers and took them to a place inside themselves where they were free.

Intro

E	E	E
		I'm gonna

Verse 1

E	E	E	E			
lay down my	burden,	down by the	riverside,			

B7	B7	E	E			
Down by the	riverside,	down by the	riverside, I'm gonna			

E	E	E	E	B7	B7	E
lay down my	burden,	down by the	riverside, and	study	war no	more.

Chorus

E7	A	A	E		
I ain't gonna	study war no	more, I ain't gonna	study war no		

E	B7	B7	E	E7	A
more, I ain't gonna	study	war no	more,	I ain't gonna	study war no

A	E	E	B7	B7	E	E
more, I ain't gonna	study war no	more, I ain't gonna	study	war no	more.	

Verse 2

	E		E		E		E
I'm gonna	put on my	long white robe,	down by the	riverside

B7   **B7**   **E**   **E**
Down by the   riverside,   down by the   riverside, I'm gonna

E   **E**   **E**   **E**   **B7**   **B7**   **E**
put on my   long white robe,   down by the   riverside, and   study   war no   more.

Chorus

E7   **A**   **A**   **E**
I ain't gonna   study war no   more, I ain't   gonna   study war no

E   **B7**   **B7**   **E**   **E7**   **A**
more, I ain't gonna   study   war no   more,   I ain't gonna   study war no

A   **E**   **E**   **B7**   **B7**   **E**   **E**
more, I ain't gonna   study war no   more, I ain't gonna   study   war no   more.

Verse 3

	E		E		E		E
I'm gonna	lay down my	sword and shield,	down by the	riverside,

B7   **B7**   **E**   **E**
Down by the   riverside,   down by the   riverside, I'm gonna

E   **E**   **E**   **E**   **B7**   **B7**   **E**
lay down my   sword and shield,   down by the   riverside, and   study   war no   more.

Chorus

E7   **A**   **A**   **E**
I ain't gonna   study war no   more, I ain't   gonna   study war no

E   **B7**   **B7**   **E**   **E7**   **A**
more, I ain't gonna   study   war no   more,   I ain't gonna   study war no

A   **E**   **E**   **B7**   **B7**   **E**
more, I ain't gonna   study war no   more, I ain't gonna   study   war no   more.